A STYLE MANUAL FOR STUDENTS

A STYLE MANUAL
FOR STUDENTS

———

EDWARD D. SEEBER

*for the preparation of
term papers, essays, and theses*

Indiana University Press
Bloomington & London

TO THE STUDENT

This guide for authors of term papers, essays, and theses explains and illustrates present-day styling, footnoting, bibliographical procedure, typing, and other matters indispensable for the achievement of correctness, clarity, ease of reading, consistency, and good appearance.

It also corresponds in the main with the *MLA Style Sheet*, which has been influential in simplifying and regularizing the scholarly style of many American journals and university presses. At the same time, its sphere of usefulness extends by design beyond the humanities, even though it does not deal expressly with certain usages, especially as regards footnote citation, peculiar to some other fields. It is not dogmatic, but makes appropriate allowances for personal choice between correct alternatives, and for usages that may be prescribed or favored by a particular department or school.

Taking a realistic view of students' needs, this manual avoids unwarranted and confusing distinctions between the styling of papers or theses and the preparation of manuscripts for publication. It thus provides a useful guide to principles that can be applied, with minor adjustments, to the styling of printers' copy. A similar volume, *A Style Manual for Authors*, contains additional information of use to writers of books or of articles for scholarly journals.

Bloomington, Indiana
March 1964

CONTENTS

A STYLE MANUAL FOR STUDENTS

I

GENERAL SUGGESTIONS

1 **Identical copy.** Retain an extra and *identical* copy of your typescript, containing all corrections, inserts, and other alterations.

2 **Copyreading.** Copyread your manuscript carefully (whether you do your own typing or not), checking for accuracy and consistency in usage and style, word division, punctuation, spacing, etc. Complete and verify all quotations as regards source, spelling, punctuation, accent marks, etc.

3 **Revision.** Allow some time to elapse, if possible, between your first and final drafts. Before submission, try to eliminate pompous and pedantic diction, clichés, digressions and irrelevancies, ambiguities and omissions in footnotes, unsuitable abbreviations in the text proper,* colloquialisms, meaningless words, circumlocutions, and repetitious words, phrases, or subject matter. Reduce so far as possible the number of your footnotes and lengthy quotations. Consult your dictionary frequently.

4 **Consistency.** To achieve consistency, keep before you a list of your spellings of variable proper nouns and words like

---

* Among those to be avoided in the text are abbreviations of months (Feb.), MS for manuscript, except in references (do not say "this MS," but "MS. 16" is permissible), U.S., St. (Street), Jas. (James), Rev. ("the Rev. Jones"), Vol., p., 1st. Allowed are: Mr., Dr., St. (Saint), A.D., A.M., i.e., e.g., etc., viz., and, in parenthetical references, Vol., p., vv., cf., and the like.

role—rôle, co-ordinate—coördinate—coordinate, traveled—
travelled, wilful—willful, sizable—sizeable, per cent—per-
cent; also forms like Mar.—March, April 1940—April, 1940,
& Co.—and Co., p. 24 n.—p. 24n., Chap.—chap.—ch., etc.
Note the use of required or optional capitals with words
relating to religious denominations or sects, philosophical,
literary, or artistic schools: Baptist, Epicurean, epicurean,
Romantic Movement, romanticism, Naturalism, naturalist,
Pre-Raphaelites, etc.

5 Corrections. If it is permissible in informal papers and reports to make last-minute corrections and insertions, these
may be written (typed, if you do not write legibly) *above*
the line (not in margins) or pasted (not pinned or clipped)
to the page. Do not use proofreaders' marks. Number added
footnotes "6a," etc. Indicate precisely where insertions are
to be made, using a caret ($_\wedge$) below the line rather than a
virgule (/)—also called a "slash" or "slant"—and revise
spacing, paragraphing, footnotes, etc., as required. In theses
and other manuscripts of permanent record, such alterations
should obviously be avoided.

6 First person. It is now generally agreed that writers need
have no compunction about writing in the first person. The
use of "I" is honest and straightforward, does not in itself
reflect vanity, and is superior to self-conscious and clumsy
efforts to suggest detachment—"we do not believe," "the
present writer," "this editor," etc.

7 Dictionaries. Whether you use Funk and Wagnalls' *Standard College Dictionary*, Webster's *New World Dictionary of
the American Language*, *New Collegiate*, or *New Interna-
tional*, refer consistently to the same volume.

II

FORM OF THE MANUSCRIPT

8 Paper. Use white, fairly opaque, nonglossy paper of standard size (8½ x 11 inches). Submit no copy, even a rough draft, on onionskin paper.

For term papers and reports, a good bond paper of adequate body is satisfactory. A thesis may require one original and as many as three carbon copies, the appearance of which will be determined by the paper selected, the kind of typewriter used, the typist's touch, and the quality and condition of the carbon paper. A satisfactory weight of paper (if a particular one is not specified by your school) is best determined by experiment. Twenty-pound stock, often recommended, may produce smudging in the third carbon copy. Sixteen-pound paper has its advocates, as does thirteen-pound—that most likely to produce clear copies. One may consider using sixteen-pound paper for the first two copies, and thirteen-pound for the rest. Rag content should be at least 50 per cent as a safeguard against eventual color changes and brittleness. The best paper has 100 per cent rag content.

9 Carbon paper. Use only a superior grade of black carbon paper. For uniformity in appearance, discard it after typing approximately five to eight pages. Uniformity can be controlled also by purchasing at one time all the paper, both white and carbon, that will be needed.

10 Type. The common type sizes are pica (10 characters to the inch) and elite (12 to the inch). Pica is sometimes specified for theses. For appearance' sake, avoid mixed type sizes and styles.

11 Margins. Leave approximately 1½ inches at top and left, and 1 inch at bottom and right. Insert paper with left edge at zero, and set margin stops at 15 and 75 for pica type, or at 18 and 90 for elite. Center of typed page will be at 45 and 54 respectively. (These directions do not apply to some electric models and foreign machines.)

12 Spacing. Double space the text proper. Single space verse and long prose citations, footnotes, parts of table of contents and bibliography, and index, as explained below.

13 Page numbers are set one inch from top of page (i.e., on the sixth line) and flush with the right margin. Numbers (optional) on pages bearing section headings (Preface; Chapter I, etc.) are centered at bottom margin. (The table of contents is not numbered.) Write page number without period, hyphens, or parentheses.

Consider (but do not number) the title page as page i, and use lower-case Roman for all pages preceding the first page of text. After page 1 (Arabic), number consecutively to last page of manuscript. Do not number the *vita*.

14 Blank pages (except for one or two at beginning and end) and half titles between sections should be omitted.

15 Covers that are inexpensive and easily removed are suitable for term papers and the like. Some readers will object to stapling. A thesis is best kept in one or more spring binders.

III

THE PARTS AND THEIR FORMS

16 **Parts of the manuscript.** Sections of a manuscript, each of which starts a new page, are arranged in the following order:

blank leaves
title page
preface (or foreword)
list of abbreviations
table of contents
list of illustrations
list of tables
introduction
text

appendix
notes (if typed at end)
glossary
bibliography
author index
subject index
vita
blank leaves

17 **Title page** (see specimen pages 1, 2). Center all lines on page (using 45 or 54 as center guide). Type title, if one line in length, on the tenth line from top of page. If more than one line, begin on the ninth line. Use capitals only. Underline any words that would appear in italics if printed, and omit period at end. In a long title, double space between lines and use inverted pyramid form, dividing lines, if possible, by thought groups.

Type author's name, in capitals, twenty spaces below a single-line title, or twenty-one spaces below the first line of a multiple-line title. Two spaces above name, type BY or EDITED BY, centered, in capitals.

A statement of submission at the bottom of the title page

(including the degree or course, school or department, month and year) phrased according to local usage, should preserve the usual one-inch margin. (See specimen pages.)

Title pages for short papers, reports, or essays may look pretentious unless they offer additional useful information such as name of course, section number, etc.

18 Preface (or foreword) (omit in table of contents). Brief remarks addressed to the reader concerning the purpose, limits, background, etc., of the study, editions, materials, or techniques employed, a *short* list of abbreviations used in the footnotes, and acknowledgments (if any)* should be put in a preface or foreword rather than in an irtroduction (see section 21, "Introduction").

19 Table of contents (see specimen pages 3-8). All copy, including the heading, should be centered vertically on page; but the heading should not be less than ten spaces from top of page, nor should the last line be less than one inch from the bottom. Three spaces below the heading, and flush with the left margin, type the word "Chapter" (initial capital only), and across the page, ending at the right margin, the word "Page." Triple space before the first entry and between all major entries (chapters, appendices, etc.). Single space in chapter headings of more than one line in length, indenting the second line two spaces.

Align chapter numbers (Roman capitals) so that the longest begins at left margin. Each is followed by a period

* Acknowledgment of special help and favors (e.g., consultation on technical matters, the loan of a manuscript, or the granting of access to private papers) is a courtesy that cannot be overlooked; but a student may without compunction refrain from expressing thanks, however heartfelt, to his thesis director or committee for their routine work. Acknowledgments should be phrased concisely and circumspectly.

An alternate device is to insert a separate, unnumbered sheet, bearing the appropriate heading, immediately before the table of contents. If a short paragraph suffices, type it on the upper portion of this insertion, and omit the heading.

(aligned vertically) and two spaces. Unnumbered headings (Appendix, Sources Consulted, Index, etc.) begin at left margin. Leaders (double-spaced periods) should connect the last word of chapter and main headings with page number. The first period should not appear in the first space following the heading, and the last period should not appear beyond the space preceding P in the word "Page." Align leaders vertically.

Apportion entries filling two pages of a table of contents fairly evenly. Do not repeat headings on second page, but repeat "Chapter" and "Page" ten spaces from the top. Make the first entry on this page a new chapter or major section heading, rather than a carry-over line from the first page. (See specimen pages 6, 7.)

In an analytical table of contents (which should avoid extreme complexity), separate subheadings from main headings and from each other by double spacing. Indent three spaces from first word of main heading. Indent carry-over lines two spaces, and single space. Triple space before the next main heading. Type subheadings in lower case, capitalizing important words. If numbered, use system prescribed under section 49, "Outline Form." Page references may be put in parentheses, reserving page column for main entries. (See specimen pages 3, 6-8.)

20 Lists of illustrations and tables follow the general form of the table of contents. Write entries, double-spaced, in capitals and lower case; single space carry-over lines and indent two spaces. Number plates in Roman capitals, figures and tables in Arabic. For best form, consult published works in your field.

21 Introduction. An introduction, properly considered, is a part of the text and not a substitute for the preface (q.v.). In some studies, such as critical editions, introductions are justified (see specimen pages 4, 5); but in many theses they can be dispensed with in favor of a more direct beginning in

Chapter I. If preliminary matter is so treated, a suitable heading can be devised such as "The Historical Setting"; "A Half-Century of Research"; "The Ideological Background"; "Aims and Methods," etc. A historical or review-of-previous-studies approach must, of course, be confined within sensible limits. If "Introduction" is used along with numbered headings, number it also and treat it as Chapter I.

22 **Chapter headings** (see specimen page 9). Nine spaces from top of page, type CHAPTER I, centered, in capitals. Two spaces below write chapter title, in capitals, also centered. Omit period. If longer than one line, single space and use inverted pyramid form. Begin text three spaces below.

23 **Subheadings** within chapters (use these only if clearly warranted, not as mere padding) consist, in descending order of importance, of centered major headings, sideheads flush with left margin, and paragraph headings. In major headings, capitalize principal words and omit period at end. Underlining is not necessary; but if a subordinate rank of major headings is used, the more important ones may be underlined for contrast. These are usually not numbered. If a long heading would extend to the left of regular paragraph indentations, use inverted pyramid form and single space between lines. Allow three spaces above the heading and three below. Major headings may be included in table of contents.

24 **Sideheads.** Capitalize only the first word and proper nouns or adjectives, and omit period at end. If sidehead would extend beyond center of page, use two or more lines of approximately equal length, single spaced, and all flush with left margin. If these headings are clearly used for enumeration, they may be numbered in Arabic, followed by a period. Allow three spaces above sidehead, and two below.

Main headings and sideheads (but not paragraph headings) at the foot of a page should be followed by at least two lines of type. If this is impossible, leave the page short and resume on the next page.

In papers, centered Roman numerals (capitals) may be used in place of chapters to indicate broad divisions. Descriptive headings are usually omitted. Divisions indicating clear breaks in context may be shown also by extra spacing, i.e., by dropping three spaces instead of the usual two.

25 **Paragraph headings** (underlined, but usually not numbered) start at normal paragraph indentation and are run into the paragraph. Capitalize as in other sideheads, and terminate with a period or a period and dash (typed as two hyphens: - -).

26 **Mottoes** at heads of chapters begin slightly to the left of center of page and end at right margin. Omit quotation marks. Type source below text, ending at least one inch short of the right margin. Introduce source with a dash (- -) and omit period at end.

27 **Appendix.** Heading and title (which should always be given) are spaced like chapter headings (q.v.); but an appendix that fills less than a page should be centered vertically. Label multiple appendices APPENDIX A, etc., in capitals, and begin each on a new page.

28 **Bibliography.** See chapters XII, XIII.

29 **Index.** Although usually not required, a good index adds greatly to the usefulness of theses that contain complex subject matter or numerous references to proper names or place names. All entries may usually be put in a single index if it is of moderate length. If not, an author index may precede the subject index. Both are listed in the table of contents.

Heading is typed nine spaces from top of page, centered. Three spaces below, single-spaced and running from left to right margins, a note may be added explaining the limitations of the index, basis of selection of items, etc. Drop three spaces for first entry.

It is easier to type indexes in a single column, but double column is permissible. In either case, single space within each entry, double space between entries. If you use double columns, the first column should start at the left margin and the second column should end at the right margin. Lines in the two columns should be of the same maximum length, and short enough to leave a well-defined clear space vertically. Start the right-hand column two or three spaces to the right of center.

Begin each entry with a capital (except in the case of glosses, word studies, and other special forms) and use commas after entry and between page references. Omit period after last page reference. Use corrected, modernized spellings when possible, avoiding the use of "sic." The form "Chap. IV, *passim*" may be used if appropriate, but specific page references are preferred. "Passim" and other words that are not index entries are underlined (for italics). Write cross references as follows: Esquemeling, Alexandre, *see* Oexmelin; but write "see also *Hamlet*" without underlining. Write titles thus: *Scots Poem, A; Progress of Romance, The.* Footnotes may be indicated in various ways: 56n, 76 n. 3; 56*n*, 76 and *n*.; 39 (n. 16), 158 (nn. 38, 39).

Consult, on this subject, Sina Spiker, *Indexing Your Book. A Practical Guide for Authors* (Madison: University of Wisconsin Press, 1964), and the Chicago *Manual of Style*, section "Indexes." On foreign names, see below, sections 115-17.

30 Vita, in theses, should contain the following minimal information: full name, place and date of birth, educational background and degrees (with a list of professors under whom the candidate studied for advanced degrees), and previous occupations and employment. The *vita* is inserted at the end of the manuscript, is not numbered, and is not included in the table of contents.

IV

PUNCTUATION AND THE MECHANICS OF WRITING

31 Comma. Use a comma (*a*) before and after the abbreviations "i.e.," "e.g.," and "viz.," but not preceding "such as"; (*b*) to separate independent clauses (unless they are extremely short or have the same subject) joined by a pure conjunction (*and, but, or, for, neither, nor, yet, so*), noting that this rule concerns *clauses* so joined, not verbs (cf. "He finished the play in March and published it in April"); (*c*) to separate subordinate clauses that either precede or follow the main clause, unless they are short and closely related in thought;* (*d*) in nonrestrictive clauses (those that can be omitted without changing the meaning of the main clause), e.g., "His first novel, which cost him his health, was never published" (cf. "The novel which cost him his health was his best").

In series containing three or more parts, final commas before "and" or "or" are recommended for clarity (e.g., "red, black, and blue pennants"; "the *History* was printed for Ball, Taylor, and Osborn"), notwithstanding a growing tendency to dispense with them. A comma may usually be omitted in an appositive used to distinguish its principal from other persons or things called by the same name, e.g., "the poet Young," "in his novel *Ivanhoe*"; but cf. "in her next novel, *Virginia*."

* For further elucidation of this and other points of grammar and correct usage, the student should own a modern work like P. G. Perrin, K. W. Dykema, and W. R. Ebbitt, *Writer's Guide and Index to English*, 4th ed. (Chicago: Scott, Foresman & Co., 1965). Consult also the Chicago *Manual of Style*, section "Punctuation," and the index.

32 Spacing. Leave *one* space after commas, colons, and semi-colons. Leave *two* spaces after periods and other terminal punctuation, e.g., between sentences and after periods following number or letter before a main section heading. *Exceptions*: one space is more pleasing after certain forms like "p. 45, n. 6." Do not space after the first period in most abbreviations: A.D., A.M. (a.m.), N.Y., U.S., Ph.D., P.S., e.g., i.e., n.p., n.d.; but space after initials of persons (R. A. Jones) unless initials alone are used (R.A.J.).

33 Hyphen. Hyphens are used mainly

- in compound numbers from twenty-one to ninety-nine
- between compound adjectival modifiers preceding nouns (e.g., a well-known man; an up-to-date process; single-spaced lines), but not with proper nouns (e.g., a New England winter), unambiguous adverbs, especially those ending in *ly* (e.g., an ever changing scene; a hastily written essay), or modifiers that follow nouns (e.g., a man well known for his charity; a process that is up to date)
- to separate identical vowels resulting from prefixion (e.g., re-educate, supra-auditory, semi-invalid, co-ordinal; but note the present trend to write "cooperate" and "coordinate"). A dieresis over *e* or *o* may replace the hyphen (e.g., preëminent)
- to distinguish meaning (e.g., recreation, re-creation; reformation, re-formation; recount, re-count, etc.)
- in a limited number of miscellaneous compounds (e.g., D-Day, self-sufficiency, half-wit, loud-speaker, make-up, pitter-patter, un-co-operative, non-coöperation).

Bear in mind (*a*) that hyphens are optional in some words (e.g., weekend, nearby, today, goodbye); (*b*) that the trend in present-day American usage (though this is not apparent in the more traditional manuals and dictionaries) is toward fewer hyphenated words (cf. office seeker, hero worship, fellow man, cross reference, songbird, antisocial, coauthor, extralegal, nonfictional, postclassical); (*c*) that a dictionary is indispensable for guidance in the correct use of hyphens and of separate and solid words (e.g., news room, newsstand, master stroke, masterwork, water level, watermark, etc.).

34 Dash. Distinguish between a hyphen (-) and a dash (—), indicated in typing by two hyphens (- -), noting the use of the latter with dates in the sense of "to" (see page 27, line 2), and—as used here—with parenthetical remarks. Neither is preceded nor followed by a space, and a comma and dash are not used together. A four-hyphen dash (- - - -) is used where a sentence is left unfinished or ends abruptly (e.g., in dialogue), and for an omitted word or part of a word; but in proper nouns written with omitted letters, hyphens may be used to represent these letters, if known, e.g., L - - d K - - - s (Lord Kames), H - - - shire (Hampshire). If the exact word is unknown, use a prolonged dash. In titles and quoted matter, follow the original form, e.g., *Histoire de Mademoiselle de* * * *

35 Quotation marks. Double quotation marks are preferred for general use, and single quotation marks for quotations within quotations, linguistic citations, and other limited usages. Punctuate as follows: commas and periods *precede* quotation marks, including the combination (' ") at the end of a quotation within a quotation. But with single words and phrases, and in bibliographical description, the preferred form is: *deshielo* 'thaw', "A Misreading of Poe's 'Ligeia'," *"Jalousie* appears to be a . . . form of the traditional 'psychological novel'."

Semicolons and colons *follow* quotation marks. Use care in placing question or exclamation marks in relation to quotation marks according to the sense required (e.g., He asked, "Are you coming?" Is it true that "Absence makes the heart grow fonder"?). Foreign quotation marks (e.g., French or

German), which are both shaped and punctuated differently from ours, are not used with passages cited in an English text.

36 Parentheses. In parenthetical matter beginning with a capital (i.e., following terminal punctuation), the period should precede the last parenthesis. *Example*: (First edition, 1831.) In other cases, period follows. *Example*: . . . in 1840 (first published in 1831).

37 Square brackets, rather than parentheses, should enclose

- words, letters, dates, etc., interpolated by the writer within quoted matter or within titles, e.g., ". . . was a frequent visitor in his [Swift's] home"; ". . . had give[n]"; *A Trip* [in 1791] *through the Northern States*

- dates, page numbers, and other data relating to published material, lacking or incorrect in the original and supplied by the writer, e.g., [Paris], 1710; p. 149 [for 194]; [David Henshaw], *The Triumphs of Europe*

- parenthetical matter falling within parentheses. This is sometimes unavoidable, but in the commonest occurrences —e.g., (*New Verse*, XI [Oct. 1934], 8); (*The Eccentric Design* [New York, 1959], p. 10)—commas are often substituted (see section 106, sample note 28)

- phonetic transcription

- the word "sic."*

If typewriter is not equipped with brackets, they can be added neatly by hand. Although the improvised form made with virgule and underscores ($\lceil \ \rceil$) is widely favored, it is likely to result in poor spacing, especially when enclosing a single letter or digit.

* "Sic" may properly be used to call attention to errors, misspellings, etc., in quoted matter—especially if these might be mistaken for typists' errors; but avoid overuse with mere archaisms, frequent misspellings in certain classes of diaries, letters, etc.

38 Dates and numerals. Note the following forms: April-May, 1940; April 5, 1940 - - June 5, 1941; from January 1 to March 15; the 6th of July. Be consistent in using alternate forms: June 5, 1941 or 5 June 1941; June 1941 or June, 1941. If a comma precedes the year date, another follows if the sentence continues: "On June 1, 1855, he. . . ." Write "382 B.C.," but "A.D. 405," to agree with the reading "*anno Domini* 405."

Spell out (*a*) a number or date that begins a sentence, (*b*) numbers of less than three digits except dates, page numbers, connected groups (of numbers, dimensions, distances, sums of money, etc.), and numbers used in footnotes, (*c*) round numbers (e.g., three hundred, fifteen hundred, four thousand).

Use commas in numbers having four or more digits, except in dates and page numbers. Write "the 1840's" (or "1840s"), "the forties" (but not "the 40's"), "sixteenth-century poetry" (not "16th").

Inclusive page numbers and dates may be written in full or in condensed form, e.g., 162-70, 1830-35. (The *MLA Style Sheet* allows this for dates but would have page numbers through 999 written in full.) When the first number ends in two ciphers, write the second number in full (e.g., 1600-1648); when the second last digit in the first number is a cipher, write either the final digit of the second number (e.g., 102-3, 1604-5) or the entire second number (102-103, 1604-1605). Do not write "1604-05."

39 Possessives. Formation of the possessive case in words ending in a sibilant (*s, z*) is not uniform, but the following procedures may be used for consistency: in one-syllable words, add *'s* (Keats's, Voss's, James's); in words of two or more syllables, add apostrophe but omit *s* (Dickens', Simonides', duchess', for conscience' sake), also in plural forms that add *-es* to a singular form ending in *s, sh, ch, x,* or *z* (Churches', Joneses', Knoxes'). In foreign names, follow the same rule after determining whether or not the final *s* is pronounced (Solis', Mme de Genlis', Dumas's, Ninon de Lenclos's).

Avoid the possessive with titles (*"The Mill on the Floss's* conclusion"*) and, generally, with inanimate objects ("the academy's members," "the Tower of London's interior"), noting common exceptions ("a day's journey," "for appearance' sake," etc.).

40 Word division at ends of typed lines (to be avoided whenever possible) is governed by strict rules of syllabication and, at the same time, by conventions bearing upon good appearance. The right-hand margin is flexible, therefore try to avoid (*a*) more than two consecutive lines ending in hyphens, (*b*) separation of single letters (*a-bridge, man-y, é-té, a-stro*), (*c*) carry-over of two letters (*hearti-ly, delight-ed, au-be, chari-té, Zwischenpau-se*), (*d*) further division of words already hyphenated (*daugh-ter-in-law, au-des-sus, Saint-Laurent, lobens-wür-dig*), (*e*) divisions of names of persons, a first and last name, and initials and last name, (*f*) word fragments at the end of a paragraph or page. Do not divide words of one syllable or integral combinations like A.D. 825, numbers (Arabic or Roman), etc.

41 English words are divided as follows:

1. In the United States (but not in Great Britain) they divide primarily on the basis of sound: the pronunciation of the line-end fragment must be compatible with that of the whole word. Thus syllabication will often be at variance with etymology: *finan-cier, bibliog-raphy, philol-ogy, perso-nae, ambig-uous, prec-ipice, chil-dren.*

2. They may, however, divide in accordance with etymology, meaning, and sound: *biblio-phile, philo-logical, personify, ambi-guity, pre-fix, child-ish.*

3. Words sometimes divide immediately before a suffix (*wish-ing, judg-ment, blu-ish, hum-ble, social-ism*), sometimes not (*tack-ling, stop-ping, tick-lish, witti-cism, sati-rist*).

4. Double like consonants usually divide (*Rus-sian, dif-ficult*), but not always (*dress-ing, dull-ard, all-over, pass-ably*).

For further refinements, see the Chicago *Manual of Style*. When in doubt about syllabication, consult any of the latest dictionaries.

42 French words are divided as follows:

1. A single consonant between vowels (including the nasalized vowels *an, en, in, on, un,* etc.) goes with the following syllable: *co-mé-die, a-mou-reux, cir-con-ven-tion, main-te-nant.*

2. Double consonants usually divide: *bail-lant, bap-tême, tor-til-lage;* but two unlike consonants, the second of which is *l* or *r*, belong with the following syllable: *éta-blir, pro-créer, peu-ple.* An exception is *rl*, which always divides: *par-ler, mer-luche.*

3. Two consonants representing one sound do not divide: *tou-cher, or-phi-que, mono-thé-isme.*

4. The commonplace liquid sound *gn* is never divided (*ma-gni-fique, monta-gne*), but in certain less commonly used words of learned or foreign origin these consonants are divided: *diag-nostique, stag-nation, reg-nicole,* etc.

43 Italian words are divided as follows:

1. A single consonant between vowels goes with the following syllable: *do-ma-ni, li-be-ra-to-re.*

2. Double like consonants are divided: *repub-blica, at-tiz-zamento.*

3. Two consonants, the first of which is *l, m, n,* or *r*, are divided: *al-bero, lam-pada, man-dare, por-porato.*

4. Other combinations of two consonants go with the following syllable: *da-gli, antipa-sto, monta-gne, chiaro-scuro;* but consonants that cannot be pronounced together are divided: *prag-matismo, op-tare, seg-mento, dog-matico.*

5. The first of three consonants, except *s*, goes with the preceding syllable: *com-prare, Lon-dra, sem-preverde, chiac-chierare*; but *di-stributivo, e-straneo*.

6. Diphthongs containing an unstressed *i* or *u* are never divided: *giu-sto, gio-varsi, uo-mini, Eu-ropa, princi-pio*. (Certain vowel combinations can divide because they are not true diphthongs: *pa-esano, co-eterno*.)

44 Spanish words are divided as follows:

1. A word has as many syllables as it has vowels or diphthongs: *ba-úl, an-ti-ci-par-se, o-pe-ra-cio-nes, ca-lien-te*.

2. A single consonant between vowels goes with the following syllable: *i-ma-gi-na-ble, a-le-mán, espa-ñol*.

3. *ch, ll*, and *rr* go with the following syllable: *le-che, papa-rrucha, ta-llador*.

4. Two consonants between vowels usually divide: *ac-ción, in-negable, nin-guno, os-ten-toso, or-nato*.

5. *l* and *r* go with a preceding consonant: *a-blan-dar, re-trac-tación, fil-tración*; but prepositional prefixes form separate syllables: *sub-lunar, des-re-glado, a-climatar*.

6. In the combination *s* plus a consonant, the *s* goes with the preceding syllable, prefix or not: *es-labón, abs-tener*.

45 German words are divided as follows:

1. A single consonant and groups of consonants which represent single sounds (*ch, sch, ph, th, st*) go with the following syllable: *Li-te-ra-tur, Mär-chen, Spre-cher, For-schung, Stro-phen, ka-tholisch, Mei-ster*.

2. Other consonant groups are usually divided: *Hun-ger, ir-gend, im-mer, interes-sieren*.

3. If *ck* is divided, spelling changes to *k-k*: *stückeln—stük-keln*. *Tz* is divided *t-z*: *blit-zen*.

4. Compound words are divided into their component parts: *Ver-ein, Manu-script, Falsch-heit, blut-rot, ehr-bar*.

5. In foreign words, *b, d, g, k, p, t* plus *l* or *r* are carried over: *Pu-blikum, Me-trum, Ma-krone.*

46 Russian words. Russian and other Slavic words (including transliterations) divide in an involved manner that can best be explained by a person conversant with them.

47 Latin words are divided as follows:

1. A consonant between vowels goes with the following syllable (*pe-cu-nia, fi-gu-ra*) except when there is a compounding juncture present: *ab-orior, prod-eo, per-inde.*

2. Double consonants usually divide: *tris-tis, bel-lum*; but *b, p, d, t, g, c, ch, ph, th* plus *l* or *r* are carried over: *pa-tribus, ne-glectum, mi-thrax, a-phron.*

3. When there are more than two consonants between vowels, all but the first go with the following syllable (*mon-strum, claus-tra*) except when there is a compounding juncture present: *trans-gressus, post-habeo.* Words containing the combination *l, m, n, r* plus *ct, ps, pt* are sometimes divided between the second and third letters: *consump-tus, farc-tus.*

4. Two contiguous vowels or a vowel and a diphthong can be divided: *the-atrum, de-aeque.*

48 Greek words divide according to the same general principles as do Latin words.

49 Outline form (this does not apply to chapter subheadings) commonly follows this style (see next page):*

* The illustration is from an article by Harold E. Pagliaro in *PMLA*, LXXIX (1964), 45 n.

I. Expository aphorisms
II. Paradoxical aphorisms
   A. Polar paradoxical aphorisms
      1. Polar aphorisms of parallel structure
         a. parallelism of antithesis
         b. parallelism of analysis
         c. parallelism of synthesis
      2. Polar aphorisms of equational structure
      3. Polar aphorisms of comparative structure
   B. Non-Polar paradoxical aphorisms

Further divisions under *c*, above, would be introduced, in order, by (1), (a), (i), etc. Note that a minimum of two is logically required for each rank, i.e., I implies a II, 1 implies a 2, etc. A single heading is otherwise absorbed into the heading immediately preceding it.

V

TITLES CITED IN TEXT AND IN FOOTNOTES

50 Form of title. Take book title from title page only. Take title of article from title page of article itself, not from table of contents. Add punctuation (often omitted in printed titles) as needed to avoid ambiguity or confusion, e.g., *Sidney's Appearance: A Study in Elizabethan Portraiture.* Give a title in its original form, even though it seems wrong or at variance with common practice: retain original spellings and archaisms like *Compleat, De Foe,* French *Avantures,* using "sic" only after misspellings and other errors that might appear to be your own.

Underline (to indicate italics) titles and subtitles of books (but not the Bible or books thereof), pamphlets, plays, separately published poems (regardless of length),* and periodicals. In mentioning a periodical or newspaper, one need not treat a definite article or the name of a city as part of the title (e.g., "in the *Indiana Quarterly for Bookmen*"; "in the Chicago *Tribune*"); but bibliographical citations should read *The Chicago Tribune,* etc. Enclose a title within a title in quotation marks, e.g., *Textual Studies of Goethe's "Faust."* Do not underline punctuation marks (except apostrophes) or spaces between words (except in hyphenated words when both parts are in the same line).

* If the history of publication cannot be readily ascertained, one may italicize titles of long poems, and enclose those of short poems in quotation marks.

51 Poems, articles, theses, etc. Titles of poems not published separately, articles, chapters, sections or essays in a volume by several authors, and unpublished theses are enclosed in quotation marks and not underlined. Book titles that figure in such titles are underlined, e.g., "Plutarch and Rousseau's First *Discours*."

52 Names of series or particular editions are not underlined and need not be in quotation marks. (See section 106, sample notes 9, 10.)

53 English titles. Capitalize all words except prepositions, conjunctions, and articles, unless one of these is the first or the last word (the longer prepositions, like "toward," are sometimes capitalized). Capitalize any word following a colon. Usage varies as regards hyphenated compounds, and not all writers observe the Chicago *Manual of Style* rule that only nouns and proper adjectives, in the second component, are capitalized (e.g., *High-Speed Trains*; but *Fifty-first Street, English-speaking Peoples*, etc.). Hyphenated words that are considered to be one word rather than a compound are often capitalized as follows: *"If"-clauses, Dumb-show, the A-text, Gold-mine, Well-being, Self-scrutiny,* etc.

54 French and Italian titles allow great latitude as regards capitalization. Follow these acceptable rules for consistency. Capitalize an initial article, the noun following, and an adjective that may come between, e.g., *Les Femmes savantes; Le Grand Dictionnaire géographique; La Revue du mois; Studi mediolatini e volgari; Piccolo Mondo antico.* A noun used metaphorically may be capitalized, e.g., *Le Rouge et le Noir; La République des Lettres.* If a title begins with a word other than an article or an adjective, subsequent words (with the exception of proper nouns) are not capitalized, e.g., *De l'amitié; Sur la pierre blanche; Sull'oceano; Alle porte d'Italia.* See other examples below, chapters XI, "Sample

Footnote References," and XIII, "Sample Bibliography Entries."

55 Spanish titles. Capitalize the first word only, e.g., *La verdad sospechosa; Amor con vista.*

56 German titles. Capitalize all nouns, e.g., *Weckherlin, zur Kenntnis seines Lebens in England.* See other examples below, section 120, paragraphs 2, 3, 4, 7.

57 Greek and Latin titles. Capitalize the first word only, also proper nouns and adjectives based thereon, e.g., *Archivum Romanicum.* Additional capitals may be used in postclassical works, e.g., *Eikon Basilike; Pro se Defensio* (Milton); *Biographia Literaria* (Coleridge). On punctuation, see section 96.

VI

FOREIGN WORDS AND PHRASES

58 Underlining. Isolated words and phrases originating with the author are underlined if regarded as truly foreign (e.g., *aficionado, pasticcio, quatrocento, pièce à thèse, Zeitgeist*). Those already naturalized (e.g., mores, a priori, leitmotif, literati, cliché, résumé) are not underlined. The list is subject to periodic revision.*

Do not underline (*a*) quotations in a foreign language, (*b*) words or phrases quoted or used in a particular sense by an author, school, etc. (e.g., Goethe's concept of *Faust* as a "rhapsodisches Drama"), (*c*) names of foreign institutions, buildings, etc., or foreign titles preceding proper names (e.g., Opernhaus; Real Museo de Pinturas; Académie de Marseille; the Champs-Elysées; le Père Charlevoix). It follows that, except for titles within titles and a few special situations, there is no need for underlining and using quotation marks around the same word.

59 Accent marks. If your typewriter does not have foreign accent marks, add them neatly by hand (do not use typed apostrophes). Omit French and Spanish (but not Italian) accents on capitals. Supply by hand umlaut on German letters (including capitals), and the character ß if needed to reproduce quotations and titles exactly.

---

* Foreign words are no longer designated as such in some of the latest dictionaries, but they are plainly marked in *Webster's New World Dictionary* and in the older *Collegiate* and unabridged.

60 Ligatures in capitalized Old English and foreign words may be suggested thus: AElfred, OEuvres; otherwise write "waeter," "coeur," etc., without attempting to join letters in typing. Ligatures are not used in quotations from Latin, in Anglicized derivatives from Latin, or from Greek through Latin (e.g., Aeneid, Aeschylus, Oedipus, subpoena).

VII

QUOTED MATTER IN TEXT

61 Effective quoting. Quotations have important functions in scholarly writing, and some papers and theses require more than others; yet a proliferation of citations (and, as a result, of footnotes) does not in itself reflect thorough and meticulous scholarship, or good writing. A common product of note-taking is a stock of apt and tentatively usable quotations; but these must be introduced skilfully and as sparingly as possible.

Avoid direct quotations, both short and long, that contain nothing beyond bare factual content to warrant verbatim citation. Present the content, with appropriate indications of source, in your own words: it will be more succinct and readable, and will likely require fewer footnotes.

Avoid a string of quotations, all of which say essentially the same thing, as a device to prove or reinforce a point or argument.

Avoid raw, lengthy quotations that readers will find repellent, onerous, and, in some degree, a waste of time. Delete superfluous and irrelevant words and sentences (indicating ellipses), and paraphrase wherever possible.

62 Best edition. Among the various kinds of editions (first, revised, corrected, authorized, critical, etc.), select the one best suited for quoting. If a late edition of a given work is the only one at hand, citations from it must sometimes be compared with the first (or another) edition to discover important changes. Most libraries contain books unsuitable for quoting, e.g., cheap-paper editions of Shakespeare or Goldsmith published in the United States in the mid-nineteenth century.

63 Typing quotations. Run into the text, with quotation marks, all prose quotations less than four typed lines in length unless they can be typed seriatim (sometimes interspersed with longer quotations) or require special emphasis. Separate from the context quotations of four or more lines in length, drop three spaces, and single space; omit quotation marks, except those that may occur in the original. Triple space before resuming text.

Manuals of style often recommend that long (single-spaced) citations be indented four or five spaces from the left margin, or three spaces from both margins, allowing seven spaces (as in the main text) for paragraphing. This arrangement, which has some esthetic appeal and many devotees, is nonetheless troublesome, invites many short quotations, and adds only a modicum of clarity. In theses at least, given a choice, it would seem sensible to save effort and space by bringing long quotations to normal left and right margins—as many books are printed. Indent five spaces for paragraphs instead of the usual seven. (See specimen page 10.)

64 Capitalization. Although quotations must be scrupulously reproduced with respect to wording, spelling, and punctuation, it is common practice to alter capital and lower-case letters introducing them, e.g., "It is apparent that 'as they part, Hugh is angry . . .'" ("as," in the original, was capitalized); ". . . summed them up thus: 'The picture which the novelist drew . . .'" ("the," in the original, was not capitalized). Similarly the first word of a long, single-spaced quotation, introduced by a colon or following a period, may be capitalized though not so written in the original. It is correct also, in this case, to begin with the original lower-case word, preceded, at left margin, by an ellipsis sign (. . .)—a form favored especially by historians. Follow one style consistently.

65 Italics. Unless there is a special reason (as in a critical edition) for indicating the original typography, quotations from early books in which proper names, prefaces, etc., are printed in italics may be written without underlining.

66 Parenthetical references. Parenthetical source references in short prose quotations precede a final period, e.g., ". . . of his own" (p. 6). If other terminal punctuation occurs, omit period, e.g., ". . . of his own!" (p. 6) In a long (single-spaced) prose quotation, reference follows terminal punctuation, e.g., . . . of his own. (p. 6)

67 Verse quotations of a single line may be run in the text with quotation marks unless they require unusual emphasis. Two lines may be so treated, separated by a virgule (/). Longer passages are dropped three spaces and centered on page, the margin being determined in general by the longest line. If lines are of unusual length, indent five spaces and indent carry-over lines an additional three to five spaces. (For further particulars, consult the Chicago *Manual of Style*.) Use single spacing and no quotation marks unless they occur in the original. Triple space after last line.

Line reference may, if space allows, follow the last line quoted, with no period, e.g.,

Lies buried in this lonely place. (vv. 30-32)

Reference to longer lines may be dropped two spaces, flush with the right-hand margin of the quoted matter. Titles, divisions, etc., are written similarly: (*Inferno,* X, 87) or (*Inferno* X.87), (trans. B. Q. Morgan), etc. In citations from poems usually printed with numbered lines, use like numbers in the right margin. References to a particular volume may be omitted if the lines quoted can be found readily in various editions; but if line numbers or other details do not agree with editions usually cited (e.g., the Globe Shakespeare), the source used should be specified.

68 Ellipses at the beginning of or within a sentence or line of verse, quoted title, etc., are indicated by three periods. Leave one space at either end of the ellipsis sign (except next to quotation marks) and *between each period. Example*: He says that "they ignore the modern . . . trends." (Note that no ellipsis is shown before "they," where there is an obvious omission.) As pointed out above, two other forms are possible: "He says: 'They ignore the modern . . . trends,'" and, somewhat more labored, "He says: '. . . they ignore the modern . . . trends.'" A comma, semicolon, or colon may precede or follow the ellipsis, separated from the nearest period by one space.

To indicate an ellipsis following a complete sentence, or between two sentences, use three spaced periods in addition to the sentence period. If ellipsis occurs *after* the conclusion of the first sentence, leave no space before the first of the four periods (the sentence period). A space *before* the first period denotes an omission prior to the sentence period (the fourth period). *Example*: "The confusion is immense. . . . There is no rigorous measure . . . ." Since the fourth period in the latter case represents terminal punctuation, a question or exclamation mark may be substituted as required.

In extended French and Spanish texts, indicate ellipsis by three *unspaced* periods, with one space preceding and following, e.g., "La Bruyère ... soutient la même cause. ..." In Italian texts, use four unspaced periods for all ellipses, or three following a punctuation mark. No space precedes, but one space follows, e.g., "L'italiano moderno, la lingua che si studia oggi nelle scuole,... è.... una lingua convenzionale...." Do not use these patterns with incidental foreign quotations in an English text.

Show omission of one or more lines of verse or of one or more paragraphs in a long prose citation by a row of triple-spaced periods equal in length to the longest line quoted. Indicate omissions at beginning and end of verse citations as follows:

> ... The Universal Cause
> Acts to one end ....

69 Paragraphing. One need not be overscrupulous about accounting for original paragraphing. A footnote reading "pp. 18, 25" may properly refer to a continuous passage quoted in the text and broken only by an ellipsis sign. Several passages may, within the bounds of intelligibility, be so treated.

70 Titles of persons, such as Mr., Dr., Professor, are commonly omitted in references to prominent authors under discussion, scholars cited, or deceased persons, though they are appropriate in more personal references, acknowledgments, etc. The titles "Miss" and "Mrs." (also omitted by some) may be replaced by a given name. Retain conventional titles with certain eminent names, e.g., Mrs. Browning, Mme de Maintenon, Dr. Johnson, Sir Walter (Scott), etc.

71 End of page. Poem titles, incomplete couplets, tercets, and quatrains should not occur in the last line of a page, and the last line of a verse or single-spaced prose citation should not be relegated to the page following.

VIII

FOOTNOTE REFERENCES IN TEXT

72 Placement. Use care in selecting the most natural and logical place for footnote reference numbers. References to quoted matter are usually put at the end of the quotation, rather than after the author's name or an introductory verb.

73 Numbering. In a paper, including one with numbered divisions, number the notes consecutively throughout. In a thesis, number them consecutively by chapters. Multiple notes on technical textual matters (as in a critical edition) are placed before ordinary notes, and use as references lower-case roman a, b, c, etc., repeating after z is reached. These letters may *precede* punctuation and quotation marks. If used next to a regular footnote reference number, separate with a comma, with no spacing. In exceptional cases it is expedient to repeat the same reference number one or more times on a single page, or to use multiple references (e.g., *dervis*[a,b]), thus avoiding repetitious footnotes.

Raise footnote reference numbers in the text slightly above the line of type. Omit parentheses. Numbers should follow punctuation and quotation marks. *Examples*: . . . papers.[2] . . . papers.)[2] . . . papers";[2] etc.

74 Symbols. The special footnote symbols *, †, ‡, §, ¶, #, especially useful after algebraic notations or wherever reference numbers would be confusing or inapt, are suitable also for papers or works like the present manual that have few footnotes. They may be used also for certain kinds of occasional footnotes in a work that has, at the same time, a number of ordinary footnotes using numerical references. These symbols may be doubled or tripled, thus providing eighteen references; but in practice few are usually needed, for they are used in sequence only on a single page, i.e., one note on page 2 and one note on page 3 will each be designated by a single asterisk.

IX

FOOTNOTES

75 Effective footnoting. Footnotes serve mainly to give (*a*) sources of quotations, opinions, and important facts cited in the text, and (*b*) the author's comments and explanations, additional facts, editorial and critical apparatus, technical data, etc., which, though relevant, would seem labored or distracting in the text itself. Bear in mind that footnotes result inevitably in continual (and often unrewarding) distractions to the reader, and that they should therefore be used as sparingly as is consistent with need, effectiveness, and clarity.

Avoid notes (*a*) that are not strictly relevant and essential, especially sources for facts that are of common knowledge or easily verified, (*b*) that repeat unnecessarily the substance of previous notes or textual matter, (*c*) that may be combined with adjacent notes (often accomplished effectively by rewording the text, rearranging material, or grouping several consecutive references), (*d*) that can be replaced in the text by short, parenthetical references to works frequently cited,* also by remarks like "italics added,"† (*e*) that are overlong: many long notes can be eliminated or at least shortened by adding information in the text, (*f*) that are of extreme length

---

* Avoid overextending this practice to references that belong properly in footnotes. Notes in the text proper must not distract the reader or suggest that two discrepant systems of footnoting are in use.

† Use italics for emphasis as little as possible in text and in quoted matter.

or complexity (such matter, if indispensable, may be put into one or more appendices or in the bibliography).

Use cross references sparingly; usually they should point forward rather than back.

A source reference usually precedes a quotation or remark introduced by the author's name or its equivalent; if not so introduced, it may follow. (See section 106, sample footnotes 27-34.)

76 Multiple references. If a footnote contains references to several authors or titles, separate these with semicolons, e.g., Smith, p. 10; Jones, p. 2.

77 Placement. Footnotes typed at the bottom of the page are the most convenient for readers; but in a paper it may be permissible to place them at the end, preceding the bibliography. Because most theses are now microfilmed, their footnotes are best distributed by pages.

One space below the last line of text, and beginning at the left margin, type a solid line ten to fifteen spaces in length.* Drop two spaces for the first note. Indent footnote number three to five spaces. Raise it slightly above the type line (with no space following) or, if local custom permits, put it on the type line, followed by a period and two spaces (see specimen pages 9-11).

Single space within each note and between paragraphs thereof, but double space between successive notes. Begin each note with a capital (except for glosses, definitions, and quotations beginning with an ellipsis sign) and end with terminal punctuation. Carry the second and succeeding lines to left margin.

A horizontal arrangement of two or three very short notes is permitted (see specimen page 11), but none may be carried over to the next line. On pages where there are many

* This form is by no means standardized: one manual will prefer a solid line from left to right margins, another will omit the line altogether.

short notes, they may be arranged in two columns, the first number in the second column following the last number in the first column. Place the second column halfway between the beginning of the first column and the right-hand margin.

78 Overrunning page. If a note cannot be ended without overrunning the bottom margin, complete it at the foot of the next page, immediately preceding notes for that page. In this case a solid line separating completed note and text can be typed from margin to margin. Such a note should be broken within a sentence to make the reader aware of the carry-over. (See specimen page 11.)

79 Prose citations several lines or paragraphs in length are not dropped two spaces, but are run in the text of the footnote, with quotation marks at beginning and end. Intervening paragraphs begin, but do not end, with quotation marks.

80 Verse citations of one or two lines may be run in the text of a footnote; otherwise, center lines on page and omit quotation marks. Leave two spaces before and after. Source may be indicated parenthetically one space below the last line, ending approximately below the last letter of the longest line quoted.

81 First references to published books and articles should give all pertinent bibliographical details. As an aid to the reader, repeat this form at the first recurrence of the reference in succeeding chapters. The remainder of this chapter shows the correct order of details, subject to possible omissions consistent with the form and sense of a given note.

82 Author's name, written with given name or initials first, and followed by a comma. Give the fullest form used in the work cited, omitting abbreviations representing degrees, etc. In a work that has no bibliography, replace a first initial, if possible, by a given name as an aid to the reader. In the case of prominent authors (e.g., Dante, Voltaire, Goethe, T. S. Eliot), initials and single or simplified names may be used in the text and footnotes, and amplified, if desirable, in the bibliography.

If a work has several authors, give the first name, followed by "and others" or "et al." (All the names may be given if there are no more than three.) A pseudonym, when first used, may be followed by the author's real name, in brackets. For anonymous works of known or conjectured authorship, enclose the name in brackets. In the latter case, insert a question mark before the last bracket, e.g., [Daniel Defoe?].

Avoid repeating authors' names unnecessarily in footnotes. If "Max Fuchs" is cited in the text, the volume reference in the note should begin with the *title*. If the textual reference is merely "Fuchs," the note may begin with the full name, "Max Fuchs," although it may be preferable to give the full name in the text. In subsequent references, "Fuchs" alone is sufficient if no other author with the same surname is cited.

83 French names. A hyphen is regularly used between given names: M.-J. Chénier stands for Marie-Joseph Chénier; but M. R. Canat (a form found now and then on title pages) stands for Monsieur René Canat. The particle *de* may be used following a given name, but not with the last name alone (Alfred de Vigny; Vigny; but *not* de Vigny). The same applies to German *von* or *van* and to Dutch *van der*, etc.

84 Spanish names are sometimes used in the full paternal-plus-maternal form (Ortega y Gasset), but more often a name will have contracted to the paternal form alone (Juan de Valdés) or to the paternal-maternal form without the conjunction (Blasco Ibáñez). Particles are treated as in French (Valdés is correct, not de Valdés). If, in a compound paternal name, the first name is "weak," i.e., commonplace and undistinguished (this includes most names in -*ez*, and the name García), the *last* name is often used in general reference, e.g., Pedro López de Ayala may be called Ayala (or by the full paternal name López de Ayala), but not López. Similarly, in a combined paternal-maternal name that has a "weak" paternal name, the maternal name may be used in general reference, e.g., Federico García Lorca may be referred to as Lorca (or by the full name García Lorca), but not as García.

Foreign names are discussed further in sections 115-17.

85 Names of institutions, societies, agencies, etc., as given on a title page, may appear as author. See section 106, sample note 5, and section 120, paragraph 9.

86 Title should be given the first time in full, or, if extremely long, in clearly abridged form, usually after the first few words. If the complete title appears later in a bibliography, use appropriate ellipsis signs, which you may discard in subsequent notes. After the first citation, title may be further simplified. Completeness of citation will depend on the nature and requirements of the study. A first citation, if there is no bibliography, may read: [Daniel Defoe], *The Life, Adventures, and Pyracies, of the Famous Captain Singleton . . .* (the remainder of the title—over one hundred words—being omitted); if there is a bibliography: *The Life . . . of . . . Captain Singleton;* and, in subsequent citations, *Life of Singleton.* (See also above, chapter V, "Titles Cited in Text and in Footnotes.") Title is followed by a comma unless the next detail is in parentheses.

If a chapter of a book or part of a volume by several authors is cited, it is enclosed in quotation marks (not underlined), followed by a comma and often by the word "in" preceding the volume title (see section 106, sample notes 11, 12). Chapter titles in books are rarely cited.

87 Editor's, compiler's, or translator's name is given in normal order, preceded by "ed.," "comp.," or "trans.," and followed by a comma unless the next detail is in parentheses. If particular reference is made, not to the text, but to an editor's or translator's technique, critical remarks, etc., this name may come first in the reference, followed by a comma and "ed." or "trans." In this case, title of the work comes next, followed by a comma, the word "by," and the author's name. (See section 106, sample notes 6, 8, 9, 11, 13-15.)

88 **Edition used,** if not the first, is indicated in abbreviated form: 4th ed., rev. ed., new ed., etc. A comma follows unless the next detail is in parentheses. (See section 106, sample notes 4, 19.)

89 **Series name** or that of a particular edition may be omitted in a footnote if it occurs in the bibliography. Name is not underlined, and quotation marks or parentheses need not be used. A comma follows unless the next detail is in parentheses. (See section 106, sample notes 9, 10.)

90 **Number of volumes,** usually omitted when reference is to specific volume(s) or if this detail is given in the bibliography, is written with Arabic number followed by "vols." and a comma, unless the next detail is in parentheses. (See section 106, sample note 2 and remark.)

91 **Place of publication, publisher, date** are written within parentheses followed by a comma.* These items, together with edition and page reference, may be omitted singly or in combination in references to well-known and frequently edited poems and plays (e.g., *The Deserted Village*; works by Shakespeare or O'Neill), also in standard reference works (encyclopedias, dictionaries, *DNB*, etc.). Facts of publication (place, publisher, date) may be omitted, in a paper or chapter, after the first citation, unless they serve a particular purpose. In a paper it may be permissible to omit them altogether provided that these data are supplied in a bibliography; but it is a common practice in thesis footnotes to give at least the place of publication and date.

92 **Place of publication.** For clarity and to avoid ambiguity, place name may be identified by country or state:

* For alternate forms when entire reference, including title, is in parentheses, see section 106, sample note 28 and remark.

Göteborg, Sweden
Bloomington, Ind.: Principia Press
Bloomington: Indiana Univ. Press
Cambridge, Mass., 1935
Cambridge: Cambridge Univ. Press

It is often correct to list more than one place of publication (Boston & New York: Houghton Mifflin Co.) or to indicate joint publication (New York: The Modern Lang. Assoc. of America; London: Oxford Univ. Press). In some cases one place suffices (Chicago: Scott, Foresman & Co., omitting their offices at Atlanta, Dallas, and New York, though given on title page; New York: Holt, Rinehart & Winston, omitting Toronto and London if the book was printed in the United States).

Writers sometimes Anglicize foreign places of publication (Turin, Munich, The Hague, etc.), but in works dealing with European literature, or requiring more precise bibliographical description, original spellings are often preferred (Torino, München, La Haye, Genève, Londres, Francofurti, Oxonii, etc.).

Place of publication is followed by a colon if publisher's name is given, or by a comma if followed directly by the date. If place is not given on title page, supply it in brackets if known.* If unknown, write "n.p."

93 **Publishers' names** are usually given in theses and in any work that has no bibliography, and are often omitted in papers that provide these names in a list of references. They often provide essential information, as in the case of a title printed in the same year or in the same city by two or more publishers. Sometimes they are given in titles of recent date and, in the same manuscript, omitted in those presumably out of print. (The dividing date is arbitrary: one may include

* But one may sometimes avoid the pedantic use of brackets if the place is clearly implied: if "Hachette" alone appears on title page, write "Paris: Hachette," without brackets.

publishers of works printed within, say, the last twenty years, or within the copyright period of fifty-six years.)

Names should be simplified: instead of "Librairie académique Perrin et Cie, libraires-éditeurs," write "Perrin et Cie," or simply "Perrin"; "Macmillan & Co." may be written "Macmillan." (Note use of ampersand and abbreviation "Co.") Further abbreviation (e.g., New York Univ. Press) is common in some fields (including the humanities) but not in others.

94 Date is given in Arabic numerals even if original is in Roman. If date is not given on title page or in copyright notice (usually on verso of title page), supply it, if known, in brackets. If unknown, write "n.d." If conjectured, put a question mark before last bracket or write "c. 1932," etc. (See various specimens in sample notes and in bibliographical section, and additional remarks in the next two sections.)

95 Articles. The full title, in quotation marks, is followed by a comma, the name of the periodical (underlined, and often abbreviated), a comma, the volume number (in Roman capitals), the date (in parentheses), a comma, and the pagination, omitting "p." or "pp." Place of publication may be added in exceptional cases for clarification, e.g., *Hispania* (Madrid). For recent issues, the precise month or number may be included: (Nov., 1963), (Spring, 1963), in which the commas are optional; IV, No. 2 (1963) or IV, 2 (1963), though once a periodical is bound by volumes this detail usually serves no purpose. Dates *must* be so written if the periodical does not have consecutive pagination throughout the year (see section 106, sample notes 22, 23). If a periodical is published in more than one series, series number must be included, e.g., *The Library*, 5th ser., XV (March 1960), 10. The designation may also be Old Series or New Series (O.S., N.S. or, commonly, o.s., n.s.), sometimes placed before the volume number, sometimes after, e.g., *The American Monthly Magazine*, n.s., I (1836) or I, n.s. (1836).

For articles in newspapers and weeklies, give date, section number, page, and column, as needed, omitting volume number. (See section 106, sample notes 20, 25.)

96 Volume and page numbers. Write the former in Roman capitals, the latter in Arabic (except when small Roman is used for prefaces, etc.). The correct form for a work of more than one volume is III, 28-31, omitting "Vol." and "pp." (For exceptions, see title in next paragraph and section 106, sample notes 5, 7, 11.) In Greek and Latin works, comma may be omitted after both author and title. Note spacing and use of periods in the following: Cicero *De amicitia* XXVII.101; Plato *Republic* 546A; and, in biblical references, Judges XIX. 27-28 (or 19:27-28). Plays, works divided into cantos, etc., may be written similarly (e.g., *Macbeth* V.iii.22; *Inferno* X.87) or, more conventionally, *Macbeth*, V, iii, 22, etc.

The date of a particular volume of a work published over a period of years can, if desired, be shown thus: *The Letters of Sir Walter Scott*, VI (London, 1934), p. 8—*not* (London, 1934), VI, 8, for here the correct date would be 1932-37, that of the *edition*. A shorter form of this reference, when place is omitted, may be written thus: VI (1934), 8. (See section 106, sample notes 6, 7.)

In citing a single-volume work, and otherwise when no volume number is given, write "p. 11," "pp. 28-31," "Ibid., p. 5," etc. Note also: p. 28, n. 2; III, 28, n. 2. Page numbers cited from the same volume are separated by commas (e.g., pp. 2, 14, 34), references from different volumes by semicolons (e.g., I, 3, 5; II, 45).

An alternate system of notation, used in the *Readers' Guide to Periodical Literature* and in certain types of publication, gives first the volume number (in Arabic), then the pagination, then the date, as follows: *American Journal of Sociology*, 58:359-360, 1953. Use only when admissible in your field.

X

ABBREVIATIONS AND LATINISMS IN FOOTNOTES

97 Underlining. Note that the Latinisms below are not underlined for italics: this accords with the trend encouraged by the *MLA Style Sheet.*

98 Ibid. (for *ibidem,* "in the same place") is used to repeat *as much as possible* of a reference in the note immediately preceding:

> [5] Smith, *Works,* IV, 55.
> [6] Ibid., II, 21 (*not* "Smith, ibid., II, 21").
> [7] Ibid., p. 30 (*not* "Ibid., II, 30").
> [8] Ibid.

Do not use "ibid." if the note preceding contains more than one title.

99 Op. cit. (for *opere citato,* "in the work cited"), referring to one of several titles cited in a note immediately preceding or (usually) to a title in an earlier note, has fallen into some disfavor, for its overuse easily results in ineffectual pedantry. If an author's name appears in the text, a footnote reference "Op. cit., p. 5" is correct, although the simpler form "p. 5" suffices and is even preferable in annotating a compact series of quotations from the same work. If the author's name is not given or plainly inferred from the text, the form "Pope, p. 5" is recommended (here an added "op. cit." is clearly redundant).

Do not force the reader, by a careless use of "op. cit." or

notes like "Pope, p. 5," to search back more than a page or two for the title in question; instead, repeat the title or use a short title (see section 106, sample notes 3, 7, 8). *Check this point carefully in your manuscript.* Do not use "op. cit." to refer to a title cited in a previous chapter, or to repeat the title of a periodical when reference is to another author.

100 Loc. cit. (for *loco citato*, "in the place cited") may be used with or without the author's name to repeat an entire reference. It should not substitute for "ibid.," should not be followed by a page reference (here the author's name or "op. cit." would be used), and should not refer to a previous "loc. cit." unless the full citation appears on the same or preceding page. *Example*:

[16] Paul Nettl, "Goethe and Mozart," in *Goethe Bicentennial Studies,* p. 83.
[17] Thomas, p. 3.
[18] Nettl, loc. cit.

Titles must be used rather than "op. cit." or "loc. cit." when more than one work by a given author has been cited.

101 Idem or id. ("the same") may be used to repeat an author's name except in the bibliography. To facilitate reading, refer only to matter cited on the same or preceding page.

102 Passim and cf. Use "passim" sparingly: specific page references are preferable. Avoid the use of "cf." (for *confer*, "compare") when "see" is intended.

103 Abbreviating titles, etc. Titles, editions, manuscripts, libraries, and even authors cited many times may be abbreviated or otherwise simplified by symbols, key letters, etc., provided that your preface or an early footnote explains the method followed. (See section 106, sample notes 17, 18.) Periodical titles, especially those familiar in a particular field, are commonly abbreviated (e.g., *N&Q* for *Notes & Queries;* see list preceding the annual bibliographical number of

PMLA). In a paper that has no bibliography, or in any work that contains titles that the reader will possibly not comprehend in abbreviated form, it is well to write full titles the first time cited. Often it suffices to use abbreviations in the footnotes, and full titles in the bibliography. If the number of journals is large, or if abbreviations have to be devised, insert an explanatory list after the preface, or even at the beginning of the bibliography if abbreviations are used there also.

104 Some common abbreviations. Note the form, spacing, punctuation, and capitalization of the following:

abr. (abridged; abridgment)
Act IV, sc. iv (or Sc. II in a play not divided into acts)
anon. (anonymous)
art., arts. (article, articles)
b. (born)
biog. (biography, biographer, biographical)
Bk. VI, Bks. VI, IX
c. or ca. (*circa,* with dates; do not use in sense of "copy-righted")
Chap. VI (or, occasionally, vi), Chaps. VI-VII (or, occasionally, chap., chaps.; ch., chs.)
col., cols. (column, columns)
comp. (compiler; compiled by)
d. (died)
diss. (dissertation)
ed., eds. (edition, editions; editor, edited by)
ed. cit. (edition cited)
esp. (especially)
fac., facsim. (facsimile)
fasc. (fascicle)
fig., figs. (figure, figures)
fl. (floruit: he or she flourished)
fol., fols. or foll. (folio, folios)
illus. (illustration; illustrated)

l., ll. (line, lines, preferably spelled out to avoid confusion
   with numerals)
MS, MSS (MS takes a period when referring to a specific
   manuscript, e.g., MS. E)
n., nn. (note, notes)
n.d. (no date)
n.p. (no place)
n.s., or, less often, N.S. (new series; capitalize for New
   Style)
No. 6
o.s., or, less often, O.S. (old series; capitalize for Old Style)
p., pp.
pp. 25 f. (or, better, pp. 25-26; pp. 25, 26)
pp. 25 ff. (i.e., p. 25 and several pages following; inferior
   sometimes to notation of exact pages)
par., pars. (paragraph, paragraphs)
pl., pls. (plate, plates)
Pt., Pts., pt., pts. (part, parts)
pub. or publ., pubs. (published, publication; publications)
rev. (revised; revised by; review, reviewed by)
s.v. (*sub verbo* or *voce*, "under the word——")
Sec., Secs., sec., secs. (section, sections)
ser., or, less often, Ser. (series)
sig., sigs. (signature, signatures)
sig. C5^r or 5r (recto), 5^v or 5v (verso)
st., sts. (stanza, stanzas)
trans. or tr. (translator; translated by)
Vol. X, Vols. X-XI
vs. or v. (versus)
vs., vss., or v., vv. (verse, verses)

American writers often prefer the following forms to the
alternatives given in parentheses:

above (supra; ante)
and others (et al.)

below (infra; post)
ff. (et seq.)
n.d. (s.d., for *sine die*)
n.p. (s.l., for *sine loco*)
see (vide)
to wit (sc. or scil., for *scilicet*)

105 Beginning of note. At the beginning of a footnote or sentence, some writers prefer "Page," "Pages," "Line," "Lines," etc., to "P.," "Pp.," "L.," "Ll.," etc., as being more pleasing to the eye.

XI

SAMPLE FOOTNOTE REFERENCES

106 Sample footnotes. The following footnotes illustrate various points covered above.

[1]Norman L. Torrey, The Spirit of Voltaire (New York: Columbia Univ. Press, 1938), p. 58. [If both author's name and title appeared in the text, the note would begin with the first parenthesis: (New York, etc.)]

[2]John Morley, Diderot and the Encyclopaedists, 2 vols. (London: Macmillan, 1897). ["New York" might be added; but this edition was printed in England. In a commoner type of note, followed by a page reference, "2 vols." would normally be omitted; but if needed, the note would then read: . . . Encyclopaedists (2 vols.; London: Macmillan, 1897), I, 10]

[3]Diderot, II, 73-75. [Short-title form of citation in n. 2]

[4][Noël-Antoine Pluche], Histoire du ciel . . . , 2nd ed. (Paris, 1740), I, 80. [Anonymous work. Abridged title might be expanded if not given later in bibliography]

[5]Smithsonian Institution, Smithsonian Treasury of Science, ed. Webster P. True (New York: Simon & Schuster, [1960]), I, 40.

[6]Shelley, Complete Works, ed. R. Ingpen & W. E. Peck (New York, 1926-30), IV (1928), 73. [Rather full form, suggesting first reference in notes. Volume date usually omitted]

[7]Shelley, Works, IV (New York, 1928), p. 73. [Simplified form, again specifying date of a particular volume. Note use of "p."]

[8] Works, ed. Ingpen & Peck, IV, 73. [The same, further simplified]

[9] Jean de La Bruyère, OEuvres, ed. Servois, Les Grands Ecrivains français (Paris, 1912), I, 3. [Work in a series]

[10] John Robert Moore, Defoe's Sources for "Robert Drury's Journal," Indiana Univ. Publications, Humanities Series No. 9 (Bloomington: Indiana Univ., 1943), pp. 22-23. [Title within title; work in a series]

[11] William F. Bottiglia, "Voltaire's Candide: Analysis of a Classic," in Studies on Voltaire and the Eighteenth Century, ed. Theodore Besterman, Vol. VII (Genève: Institut et Musée Voltaire, 1959), p. 8. [This, and n. 12, represent individual contributions in a series or volume by various authors]

[12] Frank E. Farley, "The Dying Indian," in Kittredge Anniversary Papers (Boston, 1913), pp. 251-53. ["In" may be omitted here, also in n. 11]

[13] Joseph Addison, Works, ed. Tickell (London, 1721), I, xii. [Usual reference to an author's edited works. Cf. the next note]

[14] Thomas Tickell, ed., Works, by Joseph Addison (London, 1721) . . . . [Here the reference concerns the editor's contribution rather than Addison's writings. If both figure in several references, use the form shown in n. 13]

[15] Otis E. Fellows and Norman L. Torrey, eds., The Age of Enlightenment: An Anthology of Eighteenth-Century French Literature (New York: Crofts, 1942), p. 21. [Or, F. S. Crofts & Co. Colon and hyphen added in title. Cited in later notes as Age of Enlightenment]

[16] Margaret L. Pflueger, "The Influence of Montaigne on Rousseau's First Discourse" (diss., Ohio State Univ., 1941), p. 3. [Quotation marks with unpublished material]

[17] Bibliothèque Inguimbertine de Carpentras (hereafter called Carp.), MS. 1871, fol. 81.

[18] Carp. 1871, fol. 111. [Simplified form of n. 17]

[19]Encyclopaedia Britannica, 13th ed., art. "Paper."
[Standard works require minimal publication data. An alternate, more explicit form: "Paper," Encyclopaedia Britannica, 13th ed., XIX, 725 (or, Vol. XIX, omitting page number). If author's name is important, such a reference may begin: Thomas Babington Macaulay, "Goldsmith, Oliver," etc. References to editions after the 14th (1929), which are unnumbered, may be written thus: (Chicago, 1961), V, 25]

[20]Chicago Tribune, Nov. 10, 1943, p. 24, col. 4. [Standard newspaper reference. See also n. 25]

[21]E. E. Stoll, "Symbolism in Coleridge," PMLA, LXIII (1948), 263. [Standard periodical reference]

[22]William R. Parker, "Report of the Delegate to the American Council of Learned Societies," PMLA, LXXIII (April 1958), 30. [Unlike the regular issues, this April (bibliographical) number has separate pagination, therefore the month is added. Cf. the next two notes]

[23]Atlantic Monthly, CCXI (June 1963), 64.

[24]Deutsche Zeitung, V (Oct. 4, 1950), 5.

[25]Time, Mar. 17, 1947, p. 59. [The commoner weeklies, like newspapers, are usually cited without volume number, and parentheses are omitted around dates]

[26]Desfontaines, Le Nouveau Gulliver (1730), as quoted in Leonora C. Rosenfield, From Beast-Machine to Man-Machine (New York: Oxford Univ. Press, 1941), p. 183.

[27]R. M. Smith, "Three Interpretations of Romeo and Juliet," South Atlantic Bulletin, XXIII (1948), 60-77, after summarizing three "conflicting interpretations" which prevail among critics, rejects them one by one and concludes: "Do we . . . ?" [Illustrates source placed at beginning of note. See n. 28 for interpolated reference enclosed in parentheses; also nn. 29, 30]

[28]C. D. Locock (Poems of Shelley, London, 1911, II, 280, 529), following Mrs. Shelley's second collected edition (1839), prints them as two. [Also correct, though more troublesome: C. D. Locock (Poems of Shelley [London, 1911], II, 280, 529), etc. Similarly, a periodical reference in parentheses may be written: (. . . FR, XXXVI, 1963, 459)]

[29] He states (p. 10) that he had "heard rational men . . . ."

[30] In III, 9, he says: "London was . . . ."

[31] "Soon after his return in 1842, he was tried by a Court Martial . . ." (<u>DNB</u>).

[32] And perhaps editor-in-chief, if that is what Boswell's "engaged . . . to superintend" means (Hill-Powell, I, 307). [Or, . . . means. Hill-Powell, I, 307. Follow one style consistently. Although references in nn. 31 and 32 are put at the end (the less awkward position), the form shown in nn. 27-30 is generally preferred if practicable]

[33] ". . . a high degree of taste . . ." (ibid., p. 5).

[34] ". . . a high degree of taste . . . ." (Ibid., p. 5.) [In the last two examples, note the change in ellipsis sign, capitalization, and closing period. Follow one style consistently]

XII

BIBLIOGRAPHY

107 Placement. In published works, bibliographies in some fields are distributed by chapters, and in critical editions they often follow the introduction. In theses, they are traditionally put at the end.

108 Heading. Since relatively few studies offer in the bibliography section an exhaustive list of works by a given author, or on a given subject, the heading "Bibliography" may be both overpretentious and inaccurate. Choose therefore a more precise heading such as "Works Cited," "List of References, partially Annotated," "Selected List of References," "Selected Bibliography," "Sources Consulted," etc.

Type heading, in capitals, on the twelfth line from top of page. Begin first entry five spaces below heading, or below a possible statement explaining abbreviations, omissions, and other special features. (Such remarks, set three spaces below heading, are single-spaced and run from left to right margin.)

109 Contents. The bibliography must contain every work cited (i.e., quoted or adduced as evidence or authority) in the text and footnotes, with the exception of primary sources quoted from secondary sources, and sources of incidental allusions, familiar quotations, etc., inclusion of which would be mere pedantry. It may also contain (except under the heading "Works Cited") works consulted but not used or quoted.

For easy reference, all entries—primary and secondary printed sources, journals, occasional manuscripts—can usually be put in a single section; but a separation of disparate material (printed and manuscript sources, public documents, news articles, editorials, reports, decrees, etc.) is sometimes desirable, especially if the number of items is large. Another common division consists of works about an author, and works by the author. Division headings (if any) are centered on page, the important words capitalized (*not* underlined), with triple spacing before and after. They need not be numbered.

110 Annotation. Brief annotations enhance the value of many bibliographies. See section 120, entries Sainte-Beuve in paragraph 3 and Weintraub in paragraph 7, also the several volumes of Cabeen (ed.), *A Critical Bibliography of French Literature* (Syracuse University Press), the source of these examples.

111 Form. Begin each entry at left margin, indent subsequent lines of the same entry from three to five spaces, and single space. Double space between entries. Do not carry over part of an entry to the next page. First page may be numbered at bottom margin.

112 Author's name. Give the fullest form of the author's name used in the work listed. If possible, replace initials by given names as an aid to the reader. If desired, title-page form can be represented exactly thus: Smith, A[bner] B. If a work is signed only with initials, enter these in lieu of full name, e.g., enter A.B.S. under S., A.B., or, if name is known, S[mith], A[bner] B.

The completeness of the author entry is at the discretion of the writer. Under certain circumstances it would seem pedantic to supply the given names of, say, T. S. Eliot or H. G. Wells, or the real names of familiar writers like Anatole France, Novalis, Owen Meredith, or Gorki. Also, it would be misleading to list the well-known "Eugène" Sue under his real name, Marie-Joseph Sue.

113 Anonymous authors; pseudonyms. In anonymous works, any intimation of authorship on title page should be included (see sample entries *Literary Amusements* and *Le Mari silphe* in paragraph 10). Enter anonymous works of known or presumed authorship as follows: [Defoe, Daniel], or [Defoe, Daniel?]. Enter pseudonymous works thus: Tallentyre, S. G., pseud. of Evelyn Beatrice Hall; or, Tallentyre, S. G. [Evelyn Beatrice Hall].

114 Repeated name. To repeat an author's name, type a solid line from five to seven spaces long, starting at left margin and ending with a period. Arrange titles by a single author alphabetically (including collected works, contrary to usual library cataloguing system) unless there is good reason for choosing a chronological order. Both styles should not be used in the same section. If there are one or more titles by Arnold B. Smith, and another by the same Smith in collaboration with Tracy R. Jones, enter this title last as follows: ———, and Tracy R. Jones. (Or, Jones, Tracy R. See section 120, paragraph 5, third entry and remark.) This would be followed by works by Smith and *two* collaborators, etc. In listing like names, the simpler forms precede the more complex: Jones, John, precedes Jones, John Thomas.

115 French names are alphabetized as follows:

> La Place, Antoine de
> Maupassant, Guy de
> Montesquieu, Charles de Secondat, Baron de

In some cases the particle *de* plus the article have become affixed to the name (e.g., Du Guesclin; Des Barreaux), and

Anglicized forms usually begin with the particle (e.g., De la Mare; De Selincourt).

116 **Spanish names** in their full form consist of given name (José) plus paternal name (Ortega) plus conjunction (y) plus maternal name (Gasset). While this form is usual in some instances, most names drop the conjunction and the maternal name (e.g., Lázaro Cárdenas; Juan de Valdés; Pedro Calderón de la Barca). Another common simplification consists in dropping only the conjunction, thus bringing together the paternal and maternal names (e.g., Vicente Blasco Ibáñez; Manuel Avila Camacho). As a general rule, alphabetize Spanish names by the paternal name only, treating particles in the same way as the French particle *de*. The foregoing names would be listed as follows:

> Avila Camacho, Manuel
> Blasco Ibáñez, Vicente
> Calderón de la Barca, Pedro
> Cárdenas, Lázaro
> Ortega y Gasset, José
> Valdés, Juan de

Names like José Léon Toral, Estéban Manuel de Villegas, and Carlos Antonio López cannot be alphabetized correctly until one determines whether the second name is the paternal name, or a second given name. In a combined paternal-maternal name like Federico García Lorca, having a "weak" paternal name (explained above, section 84), the maternal name (Lorca) is used so commonly for general reference that in bibliography and indexing it is well to use cross references: Lorca. *See* García Lorca.

117 **German and Dutch names.** German names written with an umlaut (*ä, ö, ü*) are listed as though spelled out (*ae, oe, ue*). In German and Dutch names, treat *von, van, van't,* and *van der* like the *de* in Guy de Maupassant (e.g., Spee, Friedrich von), noting exceptions (Von der Mühll, Emanuel; Enno van Gelder, H. A.).

For further guidance, consult foreign encyclopedias, Library of Congress cards, Chicago *Manual of Style* (section "Indexes"), and Sina Spiker, *Indexing Your Book* (Madison: University of Wisconsin Press, 1964).

118 Details. The amount of bibliographical detail required in an entry will be determined by the nature of the study. It is usually unnecessary to enter excessively long titles, the format (fol., 8vo, etc.), authors of prefaces and introductions, or the pagination of books. Articles, however, show complete pagination as well as continuations in later numbers or volumes (see section 120, entry Henderson in paragraph 12). In a bibliography containing many titles published in one place, the name may be omitted if so explained at the outset, e.g., "Place of publication is Paris unless otherwise noted." Except in special cases, record the total number of volumes in a multivolume work rather than particular volumes cited in footnotes. (Cf., in section 120, paragraph 3, entries Channing and Sainte-Beuve; paragraph 4, entries Mirabeau and Voltaire.)

In a bibliography entry, retain the same order of details as prescribed above for footnote references; but list the author's last name first, and use periods rather than commas to separate the main parts of the entry, i.e., author, title (book or article), and facts of publication. Omit parentheses with the latter. Supply missing data (author, place, date, etc.) in brackets, if determinable, and add question marks in cases of conjecture.

Enter anonymous works under their titles, not under a section labeled "Anonymous." Retain initial articles in titles, but alphabetize under the next word, e.g., list *A Voyage* . . . under V. In foreign works, English "ed.," "trans.," "vols.," "introduction by," etc., may be used instead of their foreign equivalents. Foreign places of publication are discussed above, section 92.

For further technical discussion, see Ronald B. McKerrow, *An Introduction to Bibliography for Literary Students* (Oxford: Clarendon Press, 1928), and Fredson Bowers, *Principles of Bibliographical Description* (New York: Russell and Russell, 1962).

119 Checking. As a final and most important step, compare each title cited in your footnotes with the corresponding entry in the bibliography. Failure to do so will invariably result in omissions, discrepancies, and errors in various details.

XIII

SAMPLE BIBLIOGRAPHY ENTRIES

120 Sample bibliography entries. The following examples illustrate common types of bibliographical entry and their styling.

1. Edited or translated works:

Dante Alighieri. The Divine Comedy of Dante Alighieri, trans. J. A. Carlyle, Thomas Okey, and P. H. Wicksteed; Introd. by C. H. Grandgent. The Modern Library. New York: Random House, 1932. [Less formally, "Dante," since "Alighieri" recurs in title. Grandgent's introduction is included because of this scholar's eminence in Dante studies]

Dictionary of Political Economy, ed. R. Palgrave. 3 vols. New York: Macmillan, 1901-8. [Or, Sir Robert Palgrave, although the simpler form serves its purpose here]

Fordham, Elias P. Personal Narrative of Travels . . . 1817-1818, ed. F. A. Ogg. Cleveland: A. H. Clark Co., 1906. [Length of title warrants abridgment here]

Leslie, Charles. Histoire de la Jamaïque, trans. Raulin. 2 vols. Londres, 1751.

Teuffel, Wilhelm Sigmund. History of Roman Literature, rev. & enlarg. Ludwig Schwabe; trans. George C. W. Warr. 2 vols. London: George Bell & Sons, 1900.

2. Works in a series:

The Aufère Papers: Calendar and Selections, ed. Winifred Turner. Publications of the Huguenot Society of London, No. 40. London: Frome, Butler & Tanner, 1940.

Bowers, David F., ed. Foreign Influences in American
Life: Essays and Critical Bibliographies. Princeton
Studies in American Civilization, Vol. II. Princeton:
Princeton Univ. Press, 1944.

Judson, Alexander C. Sidney's Appearance: A Study in
Elizabethan Portraiture. Indiana Univ. Publications,
Humanities Series No. 41. Bloomington: Indiana Univ.
Press, 1958.

König, Karl. Ueberseeische Wörter im Französischen
(16.-18. Jahrhundert). Beihefte zur Zeitschrift für
romanische Philologie, No. 91. Halle: Max Niemeyer
Verlag, 1939. [Or, omit "Verlag"]

3. Part (chapter, essay, etc.) of a work or series:

Channing, Edward. The Jeffersonian System, 1801-1811, Vol.
XXI of The American Nation: A History, ed. A. B. Hart.
New York: Harper & Bros., 1906. [Essentially a
separate book, though in a multivolume work, this title
is italicized; cf. the next two entries]

Feise, Ernst. "Zum Problem von Goethes Clavigo," Studies
in German Literature in Honor of Alexander Rudolph Hohl-
feld. Univ. of Wisconsin Studies in Language and Literature, No. 22. Madison, 1925. ["In" may be used
before "Studies." Page numbers are not essential,
though some writers prefer to include them]

Sainte-Beuve, Charles-Augustin. "Les Confessions de
J.-J. Rousseau," in his Causeries du lundi, III, 78-97.
Paris: Garnier, n.d.
Excellent analysis of originality of style of Confessions:
naturalness, realism, occasional archaisms, and charm.
(Dated Nov. 4, 1850.) [Essay in a collection; annotated
entry (see also Weintraub in paragraph 7)]

4. Foreign titles:

Eslava y Elizondo, H. Breve memoria histórica de la mú-
sica religiosa en España. Madrid, 1860.

Göpfert, Herbert Georg. "Der Dichter und das Drama unserer
Zeit." Neue Literatur, XXXVIII (1937), 231-34.

———. Paul Ernst und die Tragödie. Diss., Greifswald.
Leipzig, 1932. [Published; cf. Wycoco in paragraph 11]

70

Massini Ezcurra, José M. El cancionero argentino. Santa
Fe, Arg., 1956. [Identification of place name added]

Mirabeau, Victor Riquetti, Marquis de. L'Ami des hommes,
ou Traité de la population. New ed., 5 vols. Avignon,
1762.

Restori, A. "Per la storia musicale dei trovatori proven-
zale." Rivista musicale italiana, III (1896), 407-51.

Voltaire, François-Marie Arouet de. OEuvres complètes,
ed. Moland. 52 vols. Paris: Garnier, 1877-85.

[See also Metchenko in paragraph 12]

5. Several works by one author:

Fellows, Otis E. French Opinion of Molière (1800-1850).
Brown Univ. Studies, Vol. III. Providence: Brown
Univ., 1937.

———. Review of Diderot, The Testing Years, 1713-1759,
by Arthur M. Wilson. FR, XXXI (1958), 579-81.

———, and Norman L. Torrey, eds. The Age of Enlightenment: An Anthology of Eighteenth-Century French Literature. New York: F. S. Crofts & Co., 1942. [Colon and
hyphen added. Note that second name follows footnote
style. Some authors and manuals (e.g., Chicago)
prefer to give surname first]

Gwilliam, John. The Exile of Elba: A Poem . . . . London,
[1814].

———. The Imperial Captive; or, The Unexampled Career
of the Ex-Emperor, Napoleon . . . . 2 vols. London,
1817.

6. Works by two or more authors: see the third entry in preceding paragraph, and Metchenko in paragraph 12.

7. Data supplied in brackets:

Benezet, Anthony. Short Observations on Slavery, Introductory to some Extracts from the Writings of the Abbé
Raynal . . . . N.p., [1770?]. [Or, "c. 1770," in
brackets]

[Fisher, Charles Edward?]. Kanzas [sic] and the Constitution. Boston: Damrell & Moore, 1856.

Schiller, Friedrich. Werke . . . , ed. E. Jenny. 10 vols. [Basel: Birkhäuser, 1945.] [Redundancies in titles (here, Schillers Werke) are usually avoided]

W[eintraub], S[tanley], ed. "St. Pancras Manifesto." Shaw Review, III, No. 1 (1960), 21-31. Text of a political tract by G. B. Shaw and Sir William Geary. [Annotated entry. Also correct: III, 1 (1960), etc.]

[See also British Museum in paragraph 9]

8. Descriptive, rather than actual, title:

Bowe, Forrest L. [Bibliographical notes on early American translations from the French]. Papers of the Bibliographical Society of America, XXXV (1941), 70, 72, 159-61, 205-6.

[See also the second entry in paragraph 5]

9. Institution, organization, government, etc., as author:

British Museum, Department of Printed Books. Subject Index of the Modern Works Added to the Library of the British Museum [1881-1935]. . . , ed. G. K. Fortescue and others. 11 vols. London, 1902-37.

Great Britain, Parliamentary Papers. Report of the Committee of the House of Commons in Consequence of the Several Motions Relative to the Treatment of Prisoners of War . . . . London, 1798.

Philadelphia Bibliographical Center and Union Library Catalogue. Union List of Microfilms. Rev. ed. Supplement, 1949-52. Ann Arbor, Mich.: J. W. Edwards, 1953.

U.S. Congress. State Papers and Correspondence Bearing upon the Purchase of the Territory of Louisiana. 57th Congress, 2nd sess., House Document No. 431. Washington, 1903.

10. Anonymous works:

"Daudet and Dickens." LTLS, May 11, 1940, p. 231. [Or, The (London) Times Literary Supplement]

H., H.S. "The 'Lost' Sixth Douay Diary." N&Q, CLXXVI (1944), 84-86.

Literary Amusements; Evening Entertainer. By a Female Hand. 2 vols. Dublin: S. Price and others, 1782.

Le Mari silphe, par M. F....C.A.L.P.d.T. Musique de M. Fournier. Toulouse: Jean Baour, 1775. [Probable interpretation: Monsieur F., collecteur à la porte de Toulouse]

11. Unpublished works:

Musa, Mark. "Inferno, Canto XIX." Paper read before the Renaissance Club of Indiana University, Jan. 20, 1963.

Wycoco, Remedios S. "The Types of North-American Indian Tales." Diss., Indiana Univ., May 1951.

12. Periodicals and annuals:

Cowley, Malcolm. "Footnote on French Prosody." New Republic, May 22, 1944, pp. 714, 716.

Henderson, W. B. Drayton. "Montaigne's Apologie of Raymond Sebond and King Lear." Shakespeare Assoc. Bull., XIV (1939), 209-53; XV (1940), 40-54.

Metchenko, A., A. Dement'ev, and G. Lomidze. "For a Profound Elaboration of the History of Soviet Literature" ("Za glubokuyu razrabotku istorii sovetskoj literatury"). Kommunist, No. 13, 1956, pp. 83-100. [Translated and transliterated title. Use same form (without underlining) in translating book titles]

Muirhead, Arnold. "A Jeremy Bentham Collection." The Library, 5th ser., I (1947), 6-27.

Steen, J. van der. "Vondels Jempsar en de Slang." De Nieuwe Taalgids, LIII (1959), 326-32.

Takahashi, Atsuko. "A Study of Theodore Dreiser's
Thought." Essays and Studies in British and American
Literature (Tokyo Woman's Christian College), VII
(Summer 1959), 71-102. [Model for lesser-known pub-
lications: place of origin added]

Thompson, Wade Clayton. "The Aesthetic Theory of Henry
David Thoreau." DA, XX (1960), 3756 (Columbia).
[Dissertation abstract]

13. Encyclopedias; standard reference works:

"Goldsmith, Oliver." Encyclopaedia Britannica. 14th ed.,
X, 494-98. [Or, Vol. X (omitting page numbers)]

"Gosset, Isaac." DNB, VIII, 261-62.

Macaulay, Thomas Babington. "Goldsmith, Oliver." Encyclopaedia Britannica, [etc.].

THE CHANGING ATTITUDE TOWARD GEORG BÜCHNER

BY

ERWIN LOUIS MEYER

Submitted to the Faculty of the Graduate School
in partial fulfilment of the requirements
for the degree Doctor of Philosophy
in the Department of German
Indiana University
August, 1945

THE INFLUENCE OF RICHARD WAGNER

IN FRENCH LITERATURE

(1860 TO 1890)

BY

WARREN JERROLD WOLFE

Submitted to the Faculty of the Graduate School
in partial fulfilment of the requirements
for the degree Master of Arts in the
Department of French and Italian
Indiana University
May 1949

TABLE OF CONTENTS

Specimen Page 4

TABLE OF CONTENTS

CONTENTS

Specimen Page 6

Specimen Page 7

Specimen Page 8

TABLE OF CONTENTS

CHAPTER X

THE SLAVERY QUESTION DURING THE REVOLUTIONARY
PERIOD, 1789-1794

During the last few years of the legal existence of
colonial slavery, humanitarian literature was significantly
expanded by several new works directed against the enslave-
ment of Negroes.[1] The views of the celebrated Thomas Clark-
son were presented anew in 1789 in the Idée de la traite et
du traitement des nègres and in an Essai sur les désavanta-
ges de la traite. The first thirty-one pages of the former
work contained extracts from his Latin dissertation on slavery,[2] and the remaining pages, on the treatment of slaves,
gave accounts and anecdotes of tortures and cruelties commonly witnessed in Santo Domingo.[3] The translator, Grama-
gnac, added twenty-five pages of introductory remarks. In
the same year the Abbé Nicolas Bergier published his Dictionnaire théologique, containing three articles ("Philosophes,"

---

[1] The familiar theme of the wretched South American Indians
was not, however, forgotten: see Drobecq's poem "Le Cacique et
le François," which appeared in the Almanach des Muses in 1789
(pp. 183-84); Poiret's Voyage en Barbarie (1789), I, 19.

[2] This competed in 1785 for the prize offered by Cambridge
University for an essay on the question Anne liceat invitos
in servitutem dare? An English translation, entitled An Essay on the Slavery and Commerce of the Human Species, was
published in London in 1786, and there were three French adap-
tations by 1789.

[3] The second extract "est l'essentiel d'un mémoire . . . en-
voyé à M. de Sartines, Ministre d'Etat, par un Préfet Aposto-
lique, alors dans la Colonie [Saint-Domingue]." This part
embraces 76 pages.

the authority of Simon Kenton, . . . says, 'Logan's form was
striking and manly, his countenance calm and noble . . . .'"[24]
More than seventy years later, Franklin B. Sawvel gives a similar, but embellished, description of Logan:

> Logan was now in the prime of life, a fine specimen of
> robust manhood with a commanding presence, dignified in bear-
> ing and brave as the bravest of the brave. He was built in
> the style of the primeval forest, six feet two or more, broad
> shouldered, lithe of limb and alert and as soft of tread as a
> tiger; he was self-reliant and straight as an arrow. He is
> described as handsome, with more than usual raven-trailing
> locks and as having jet-black eyes vigilant as the eyes of an
> eagle, firm-set mouth and the kindly features of a child.[25]

While these descriptions may have some basis in fact, they also
suggest a confusion with a Captain James Logan, the warrior
adopted by General Benjamin Logan--"a fine-looking fellow, six
feet tall and splendidly formed, with courage of the highest
quality" and capable of great "delicacy and kindness" to women
and children.[26] In any event, it is easy to imagine that they
are in some degree a romantic conception like that in "Lavin-
ia's" poem:

> Brave was Logan, none were braver,
> Daring war by land and main;
> Tall was Logan, none were taller;
> Hail'd the Sachem of the plain.

---

[24] The American Pioneer, I (1842), 18.

[25] Logan the Mingo, p. 67. Sawvel was doubtless aware that
Logan's Indian name (Tah-gah-jute) meant "his eyelashes stick
out or above,"--"as if looking through or over something, and
so well could mean 'spying'" (Hodge).

[26] Jacob P. Dunn, True Indian Stories . . . (Indianapolis,
1909), pp. 166, 168.

125

fable, Care (Cura) shaped a creature out of clay and Jupiter gave this shape a spirit or soul. Earth (Humus) was entitled to provide the name: a human being (Homo), according to Saturn's verdict. As to its rightful owner he decided: "After death Jupiter will receive the spirit, Earth the body. Care, however, since she first shaped this creature, shall possess it as long as it lives." ("Cura enim quia prima finxit, teneat quamdiu vixerit.")[86]

Burdach stresses the point that, according to this fable, man is "solange er lebt . . . das Kind der Sorge." But Faust has forfeited the nature of a free human being by concluding the pact with Mephistopheles. The "Uebermensch" Faust, he continues, "bleibt, seitdem er sich der Magie ergeben, frei von der Sorge."[87] "Aber," he goes on, "am Ende, nachdem er die düstere Macht der Magie innerlich überwunden, . . . steht er auf dem Weg 'ins Freie'. . . und deshalb . . . verfällt jetzt sein körperlicher Teil dem natürlichen Menschenlose, wird Eigentum der Erde."[88] By the latter Burdach means that

---

frequently that which spurs on, incites" (Harper). Stimulus even more than excitare means the spurring to some action. Gummere translates the above phrase with "routs us from our beds with the sharpest of goads" (Seneca, Ad Lucilium epistulae morales, with an English translation by Richard M. Gummere, Loeb Classical Library, New York, 1930, II, 427). The desperate deeds to which Sorge incites the rich and powerful are implied in Seneca's passage but not in Burdach's translation.

86. Burdach quotes only in German translation (pp. 41 f.). The Latin quotation is taken from Heidegger, p. 198.

87. Page 44.   88. Page 45.

INDEX

Unless otherwise indicated, references are to numbered sections rather than to page numbers.

Numerals
  comma with, 38
  inclusive, 38
  when spelled out, 38
  see also Numbers, page

Op. cit., 99, 100
o.s., 95, 104
Outline form, 49

p., pp., 3 n., 95, 96, 104, 105
Pagination
  of manuscript, 13
  of reference matter, 66, 67, 95, 96, 118
Pamphlet titles, how cited, 50
Paper for typescripts, 8
Paragraph headings, 25
Paragraphing
  in extended quotations, omitted, 69
  in quoted matter, 63
Parenthesis with period, 36, 66
Parenthetical references, 36, 66, 67, 80
Parts of the manuscript, 16
passim, 29, 102
Period
  with parenthesis, 36
  spacing after, 32
Periodicals
  cited in bibliography, 118
  cited in footnotes, 81, 82, 95, 96
  titles of
    abbreviated, 103
    how cited, 50

Place of publication
  in bibliography, how cited, 118
  in footnotes, how cited, 91-92
  foreign, how treated, 92
Plays
  bibliographical data omitted, 91
  references to, how cited, 96
  titles of, how cited, 50
P.M., *see* A.M.
Poems
  bibliographical data omitted, 67, 91
  ellipsis in, 68
  line numbers, how used, 67
  parenthetical source references to, 67
  titles of, how cited, 50, 51, 96
  how typed, 67, 80, specimen page 10
Possessives, how written, 39
Preface
  contents of, 18
  placement, 16
Proper names, *see* Initials; Names, proper
Prose quotations
  parenthetical source references in, 66
  how typed, 63, 79, specimen pages 9-11
  see also Ellipsis
Pseudonymous works, how cited, 82, 112, 113

Publishers' names
  how cited, 91, 93
  omission of, 91, 93

Quotation marks
  double, 35, 79
  foreign, 35
  punctuation with, 35
  single, 35
Quoted matter
  accuracy in, 2
  best edition for, 62
  effective use of, 61
  how typed, 63, 79, 80, speci-
    men pages 9-11
  see also Poems; Prose quota-
    tions

Reference indexes, *see* Foot-
    note references in text
Reviews, how cited, 120 par. 5
Revision of manuscript, 3, 5
Russian, word division in, 46

Secondary sources, how cited,
    106 n. 26
Semicolon, spacing after, 32
ser., 95, 104
Series title, how cited, 52, 89
sic
  use of, 37 n., 50
  how written, 37
Sideheads, 24
Spacing
  after punctuation, 32
  single and double, 12
Spanish
  ellipsis in, 68

Spanish—*Cont.*
  proper names, how written,
    58, 84, 116
  titles, capitalization of, 55
  word division in, 40, 44
Spelling, consistency in, 4
Square brackets, *see* Brackets
Subheadings, *see* Chapter
Syllabication, *see* Words, di-
    vision of
Symbols as footnote references,
    74

Table of contents
  form of, 19, specimen pages
    3-8
  preface and *vita* omitted in,
    18, 30
Tables, list of, 20
Theses, unpublished, how
    cited, 51, 120 par. 11
Title page, form of, 17, speci-
    men pages 1, 2
Titles
  abbreviations of, 18
  abridged, 86, 106 nn. 3, 4, 7
  capitalization of
    English, 53
    French, 54
    German, 56
    Greek, 57
    Italian, 54
    Latin, 57
    Spanish, 55
  correct citation of, 50-52
  descriptive, 120 par. 8
  in footnotes, 86